my travel adventures

THIS BOOK BELONGS TO

....

only sleep once more

THAT IS WHERE WE ARE TRAVELING THIS TIME:

THEN STARTS OUR TRIP

THEN WE COME BACK

I REALLY WANT TO EXPERIENCE THAT:

I LOOK FORWARD TO THAT:

I DON'T WANT TO DO THAT:

This is how I envision our vacation trip

Have I forgotten anything ?

Finally we are off

We will travel with (please tick)

That's how many miles we travel (my parents say)

. . . .

THAT'S HOW MANY HOURS
WE WILL BE ON THE ROAD.
(FOR EACH HOUR
ONE POINT.)

AS LONG AS WE WERE
REALLY ON THE WAY
(MARKS FOR EACH HOUR
A POINT.)

I'm so bored...

IF YOU ARE REALLY THAT BORED, THEN

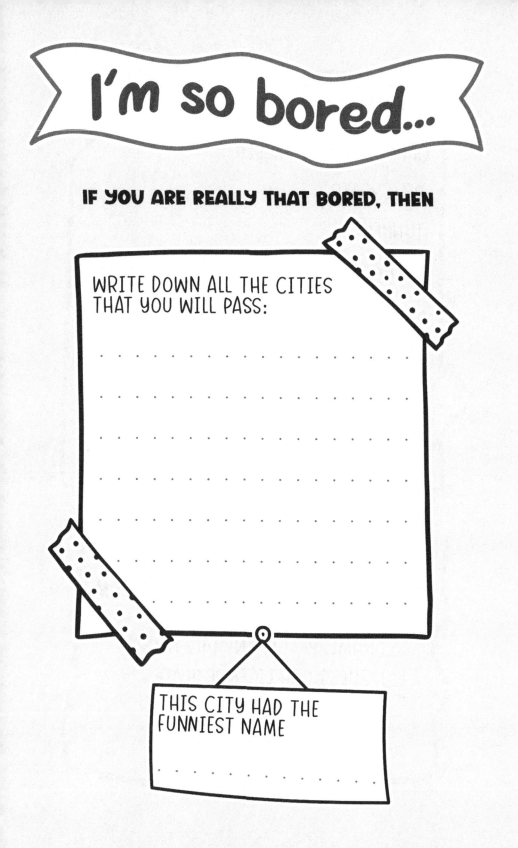

WRITE DOWN ALL THE CITIES
THAT YOU WILL PASS:

THIS CITY HAD THE
FUNNIEST NAME

COUNT IT:

CARS YOU HAVE PASSED . . . .

PEE BREAKS . . . .

TUNNEL . . . .

BRIDGES . . . .

PETROL STATIONS . . . . . .

ANIMALS . . . .

WITH THIS WE CAN PASS THE BOREDOM

- ☐ NAME, PLACE, ANIMAL, THING
- ☐ GUESS CAR LICENSE PLATE
- ☐ CAN YOU SEE WHAT I SEE
- ☐ GUESS ANIMAL SOUNDS

DRAW A PICTURE OF HOW IT LOOKS LIKE AT YOUR PLACE RIGHT NOW.

U	Y	A	S	V	D	S	E	Y	A
C	E	L	B	R	X	W	P	R	B
T	R	K	I	K	L	T	N	M	K
S	A	B	K	D	O	G	T	O	Q
J	B	R	M	T	B	F	J	N	N
X	B	P	H	S	L	C	R	K	R
R	I	Z	M	L	Z	N	B	E	O
P	T	X	H	D	G	Z	P	Y	I
G	I	R	W	P	C	A	T	Q	Z
W	K	G	B	O	Z	J	B	G	B

BIRD
DOG
RABBIT

CAT
MONKEY

U	L	U	M	Q	M	B	Y	Y	N
S	C	A	T	O	S	L	K	M	I
V	V	V	I	B	H	D	T	K	Y
C	K	K	Q	A	E	O	A	W	I
N	P	A	B	F	E	G	E	S	U
I	J	N	E	F	P	S	I	Q	Y
U	E	P	I	T	R	V	Z	P	V
N	C	Y	Z	O	R	S	M	V	N
N	I	D	H	L	X	X	X	Y	Z
D	M	A	R	A	B	B	I	T	K

CAT
HORSE
SHEEP

DOG
RABBIT

J	W	G	W	D	E	L	F	G	K
A	Z	R	C	J	H	G	O	O	E
V	A	C	A	T	I	O	N	J	J
C	Y	L	P	O	O	L	N	B	I
H	S	X	N	Z	J	U	Q	R	K
E	R	N	L	F	S	W	D	Z	G
Q	F	H	O	L	I	D	A	Y	T
Q	B	C	A	R	A	V	A	N	N
M	T	Z	K	S	P	L	H	O	L
U	I	T	Q	M	S	U	C	X	E

CARAVAN
POOL
VACATION

HOLIDAY
SUN

R	U	Z	V	K	B	T	D	U	E
C	W	E	H	B	J	W	Q	N	G
R	C	I	A	U	N	Z	O	N	X
S	K	P	D	C	M	T	I	W	S
C	M	R	T	K	S	W	R	H	Z
H	J	B	R	E	S	Q	T	Y	B
W	E	P	E	T	C	Y	N	B	C
J	Q	H	E	A	D	N	O	E	I
B	U	C	L	I	M	B	I	N	G
Z	W	H	D	X	H	H	O	T	I

BUCKET
STONE
TREE

CLIMBING
SWING

1

7	6						8	9
	9		7	6				1
	1	8	4			5		
					7	2		4
	7	1	2	9	4			
		4	3	1				8
				4	3	7		
9			6			1	5	3
5				6		1		

2

7							5	3
6				2		4		
		4		6	1			
			2	3	4			1
	9	8			7			
			5			3	6	7
	6			5			9	2
1		3	8			5		
9	8		4	7	2	1		

3

9	5	7		1				
						1	7	3
			6	8	7	9	2	
			3		5	2	6	
		2		9		5		
	1	5			8			
	6		7				3	9
5				6		7		
1	7		9					4

4

7	4	1				2		
		9		5		1	3	8
			1	6	2			
6	9		7		5	4		
			6			9		5
5			7			1	4	
	7		3					1
			5	9		3		
	1	8					9	4

5

3	4	8	6		1			
		9	3	5	2			
						6	3	7
			2	3				
	9		8			1	7	3
	3	7				5		8
4			9	1		2		8
2	7			6				4
9				3	4			

6

						8	6	4
	7	3			5			7
1			4			2	9	
				5			4	
	5		1		8	9	7	
9	4			3			1	5
			3	9	1			6
2	1	7						
		9	2			5		

7

	9				6		7	
	7					3	2	
	1		8			4		5
7		1	1		8	7	6	2
7		1	6	2			5	4
		4	9					
5					9		4	7
			2	8				
2	3	9				5		1

8

6	7	5		1		9		
	9					1	2	3
			4	8				
7	3		9	4				
1			7			4	3	
4		2	5					1
	1	3			7			2
2		7						1
		8			2		7	5

9

		6	4		1			
		5	9					2
		3		6		4		9
1	8				5	7		
9	3		1			5	4	8
			2	4				1
7	2					8	5	
5		1		3		2		
3					7			

10

6	3			5				8
9					6	7		5
			9		7		1	6
					6	8		4
5	2	3				1		
			1	7	5	9		
	5	1				6	2	
		2		3	9		7	
		6	5		2			

11

			1			3		2
2	1	9			6	8		
4	6				7			
	2	1		6			4	
			7	3				9
		4		2		7	8	
3	7		6			2		8
8	4		5		3		1	
			8					5

12

5							8	
3				6	4	9		2
6	1			2	8	5	7	
		3	2				6	
	6	7	8			2		
		2	7			1	3	9
	8	6					5	
	3					7		4
			3	1	9	6		

13

		2	3			1		5
4	2			6	9	3		
9						6		4
			1	8			4	2
	8	1			5			
		6	3		2		8	
1						4		6
	7		8	5			3	
5	3		9	4				

14

6		3		2	4	7		
		8	1		5	6		2
4			9		7			8
			5	2				6
	4			1		8	5	
1			6			4		
5		2		9			8	
8					6		7	5
		9	5					

15

		3			8	7		6
			9	6			3	1
7	4	6						9
	1		2	9				8
2	7		1				4	3
	8	4			5			
8						9		
9		1	7		4	3		
			1			8	6	

16

	4			9	6		2	7
2		9			5			
		5			7			9
8	6			2			1	
	2		7	5			3	
5				1	3	8	4	
			3			4	7	8
7		4						
9			4			2		3

17

4		1	3	6				
6			2	5			9	
	5	3		1			4	2
5		6	4		7			
	4					3	2	5
1	8	2	9				6	4
					1	9		8
			6	7	3	2		
3	1	5						

18

		2	1	6	7			5
		5					1	9
		1				7		2
9		4			1		7	
6							8	
3				2	9			6
	4		2	7		5		
	7			1		6		4
	8	6	4				9	

19

	2	8		6				
		7		4		5	6	
				1	7	8	4	
6		5			2		7	
8					6		5	4
2			4		3			
5			6			4	1	
			5			9		8
	8	3	7		4			

20

	3			7				
					4			8
9	4			2	8		6	
	6		7	1		5		
5			8	4		6	7	
4	8		5			3		1
7	1	3					4	
	4				6		9	3
	6		4				1	

21

	2	4				9		
		6	3			1	8	
		3		7	6	5		
	7		6	9		4	3	1
4	5					6	2	
			8	2	4			
				3				7
8			2	6				9
9		2		4				6

22

				6			3	8
		3	9	1		6		
6		7		8				
4	2		1			9		
	1		3		8			7
7						1	4	5
1			4		2	7		
9	7					5	2	1
3		2					9	4

23

7				2	5			
		9			4	8	2	3
4		8					1	
			1	3		6		
9		3	4	8			5	
	1			6		4		7
	9		7					1
1	7		6		2			9
		2	9			3		6

24

9	3	2						
	1			4			5	3
	5			3	8		7	
		1			2	9	8	4
	9		3					2
2			7		4			
			5			4		
5			4	1	3	6		
7		6	8				3	

DATE: . . . .

LOCATION: . . . .

WEATHER °F

THAT'S WHAT I EXPERIENCED TODAY:

. . . .

THAT'S WHAT I SEEN TODAY:

. . . .

THIS IS WHAT I ATE TODAY:

. . . .

DRAW WHAT YOU HAVE EXPERIENCED TODAY:

OR INSERT PHOTOS, ENTRY CARDS OR STAMPS

MY FAVORITE MEMORY TODAY

. . . .

. . . .

I AM GRATEFUL FOR THAT TODAY

. . . .

. . . .

THIS IS HOW MY DAY WAS TODAY

DATE: . . . .

LOCATION:

. . . .

. . . .

WEATHER . . . . °F

THAT'S WHAT I EXPERIENCED TODAY:

. . . .

. . . .

. . . .

THAT'S WHAT I SEEN TODAY:

. . . .

. . . .

. . . .

THIS IS WHAT I ATE TODAY:

. . . .

. . . .

. . . .

DRAW WHAT YOU HAVE EXPERIENCED TODAY:

OR INSERT PHOTOS, ENTRY CARDS OR STAMPS

MY FAVORITE MEMORY TODAY

. . . .

. . . .

I AM GRATEFUL FOR THAT TODAY

. . . .

. . . .

THIS IS HOW MY DAY WAS TODAY

DATE: . . . .

WEATHER 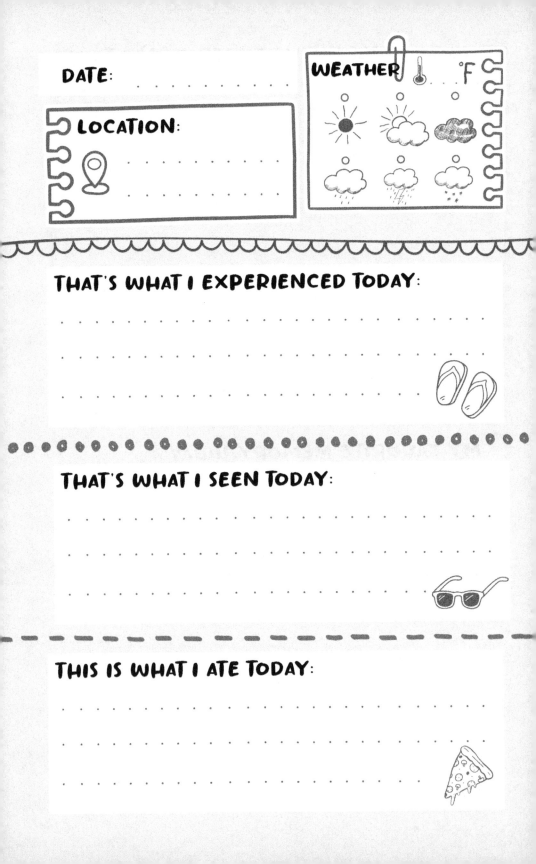 . . . °F

LOCATION: . . . .

THAT'S WHAT I EXPERIENCED TODAY:

. . . .

. . . .

. . . .

THAT'S WHAT I SEEN TODAY:

. . . .

. . . .

. . . .

THIS IS WHAT I ATE TODAY:

. . . .

. . . .

. . . .

DRAW WHAT YOU HAVE EXPERIENCED TODAY:

OR INSERT PHOTOS, ENTRY CARDS OR STAMPS

MY FAVORITE MEMORY TODAY

. . . .

. . . .

I AM GRATEFUL FOR THAT TODAY

. . . .

. . . .

THIS IS HOW MY DAY WAS TODAY

DATE: . . . .

LOCATION: . . . .

WEATHER . . . . °F

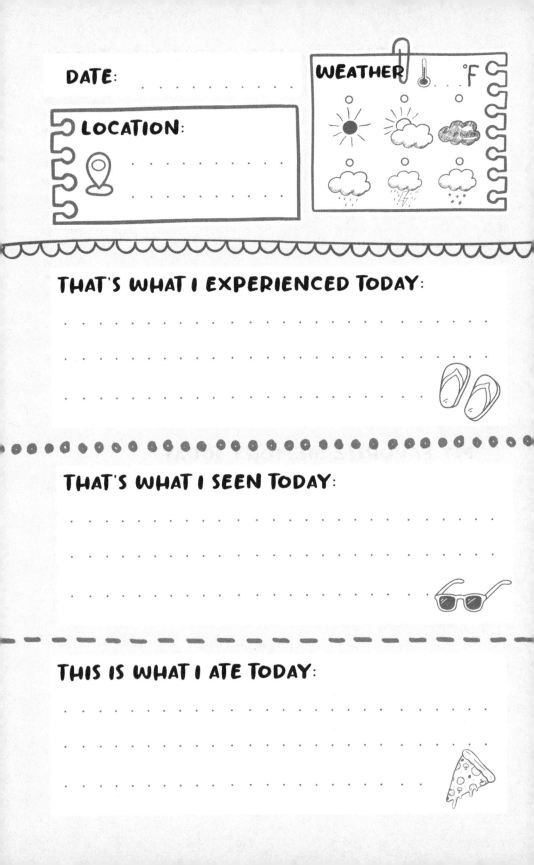

THAT'S WHAT I EXPERIENCED TODAY:

THAT'S WHAT I SEEN TODAY:

THIS IS WHAT I ATE TODAY:

DRAW WHAT YOU HAVE EXPERIENCED TODAY:

OR INSERT PHOTOS, ENTRY CARDS OR STAMPS

MY FAVORITE MEMORY TODAY

· · · · · · · · · · · · · · ·

I AM GRATEFUL FOR THAT TODAY

· · · · · · · · · · · · · · ·

THIS IS HOW MY DAY WAS TODAY

DATE: . . . .

WEATHER 🌡 . . . °F

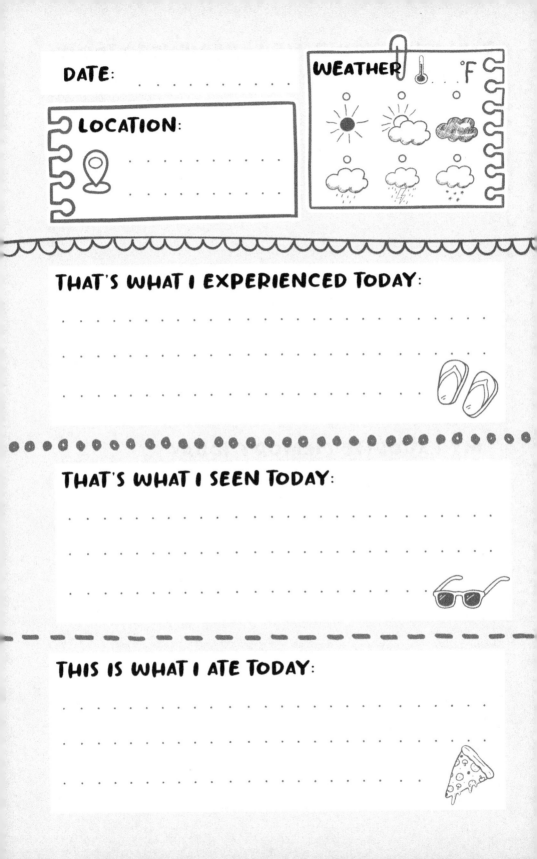

LOCATION: . . . .

THAT'S WHAT I EXPERIENCED TODAY:

THAT'S WHAT I SEEN TODAY:

THIS IS WHAT I ATE TODAY:

DRAW WHAT YOU HAVE EXPERIENCED TODAY:

OR INSERT PHOTOS, ENTRY CARDS OR STAMPS

MY FAVORITE MEMORY TODAY

. . . .

. . . .

I AM GRATEFUL FOR THAT TODAY

. . . .

. . . .

THIS IS HOW MY DAY WAS TODAY

DATE: . . . .

WEATHER  °F

LOCATION: . . . .

THAT'S WHAT I EXPERIENCED TODAY:

. . . .

. . . .

. . . .

THAT'S WHAT I SEEN TODAY:

. . . .

. . . .

. . . .

THIS IS WHAT I ATE TODAY:

. . . .

. . . .

. . . .

DRAW WHAT YOU HAVE EXPERIENCED TODAY:

OR INSERT PHOTOS, ENTRY CARDS OR STAMPS

MY FAVORITE MEMORY TODAY

. . . .

. . . .

I AM GRATEFUL FOR THAT TODAY

. . . .

. . . .

THIS IS HOW MY DAY WAS TODAY

DATE: . . . .

WEATHER 🌡 . . . °F

LOCATION:

📍 . . . .

. . . .

THAT'S WHAT I EXPERIENCED TODAY:

. . . .

. . . .

. . . .

THAT'S WHAT I SEEN TODAY:

. . . .

. . . .

. . . .

THIS IS WHAT I ATE TODAY:

. . . .

. . . .

. . . .

DRAW WHAT YOU HAVE EXPERIENCED TODAY:

OR INSERT PHOTOS, ENTRY CARDS OR STAMPS

MY FAVORITE MEMORY TODAY

. . . .

. . . .

I AM GRATEFUL FOR THAT TODAY

. . . .

. . . .

THIS IS HOW MY DAY WAS TODAY

DATE: . . . .

WEATHER 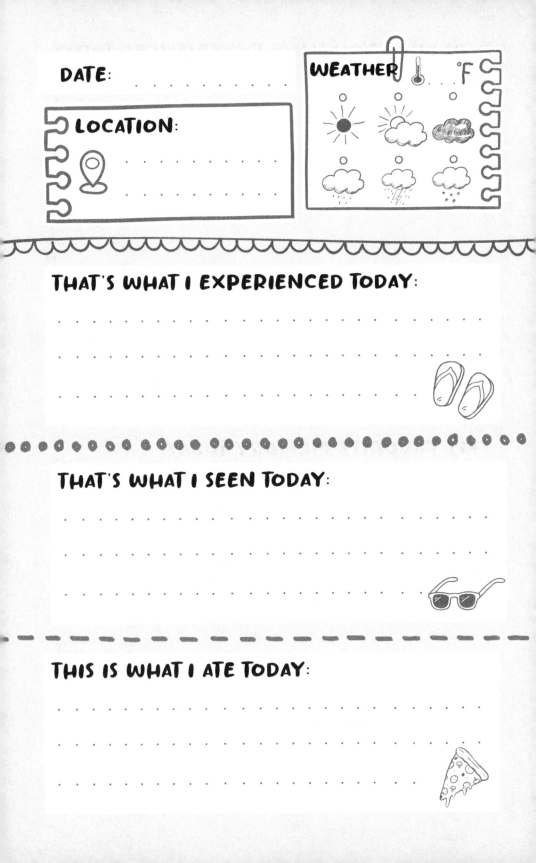 . . . . °F

LOCATION: . . . .

THAT'S WHAT I EXPERIENCED TODAY:

. . . .

. . . .

. . . .

THAT'S WHAT I SEEN TODAY:

. . . .

. . . .

. . . .

THIS IS WHAT I ATE TODAY:

. . . .

. . . .

. . . .

DRAW WHAT YOU HAVE EXPERIENCED TODAY:

OR INSERT PHOTOS, ENTRY CARDS OR STAMPS

MY FAVORITE MEMORY TODAY

. . . .

I AM GRATEFUL FOR THAT TODAY

. . . .

. . . .

THIS IS HOW MY DAY WAS TODAY

DATE: . . . .

WEATHER 🌡️ . . . . °F

LOCATION:
. . . .

THAT'S WHAT I EXPERIENCED TODAY:

. . . .

. . . .

. . . .

THAT'S WHAT I SEEN TODAY:

. . . .

. . . .

. . . .

THIS IS WHAT I ATE TODAY:

. . . .

. . . .

. . . .

DRAW WHAT YOU HAVE EXPERIENCED TODAY:

OR INSERT PHOTOS, ENTRY CARDS OR STAMPS

MY FAVORITE MEMORY TODAY

. . . .

. . . .

I AM GRATEFUL FOR THAT TODAY

. . . .

. . . .

THIS IS HOW MY DAY WAS TODAY

DATE: . . . .

WEATHER 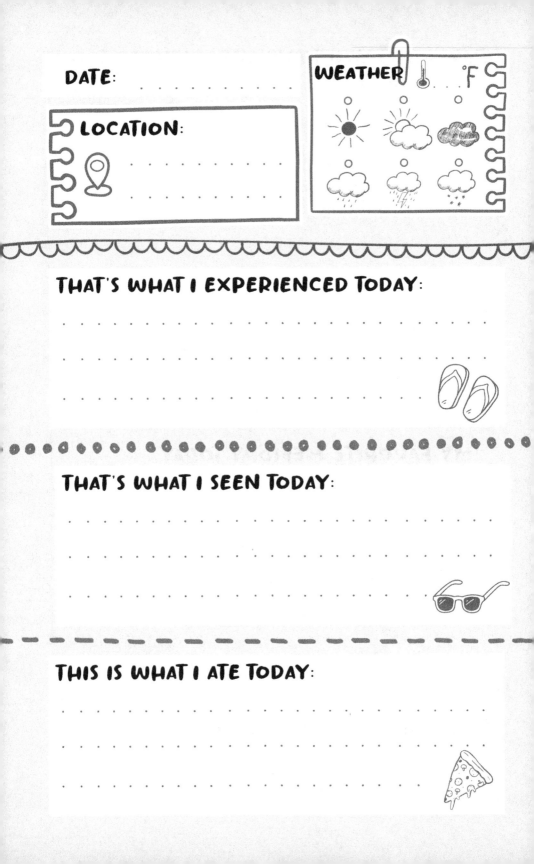 . . . °F

LOCATION: . . . .

. . . .

THAT'S WHAT I EXPERIENCED TODAY:

. . . .

. . . .

. . . .

THAT'S WHAT I SEEN TODAY:

. . . .

. . . .

. . . .

THIS IS WHAT I ATE TODAY:

. . . .

. . . .

. . . .

DRAW WHAT YOU HAVE EXPERIENCED TODAY:

OR INSERT PHOTOS, ENTRY CARDS OR STAMPS

MY FAVORITE MEMORY TODAY

. . . .

I AM GRATEFUL FOR THAT TODAY

. . . .

. . . .

THIS IS HOW MY DAY WAS TODAY

DATE: . . . .

WEATHER 🌡 . . . °F

LOCATION: . . . .

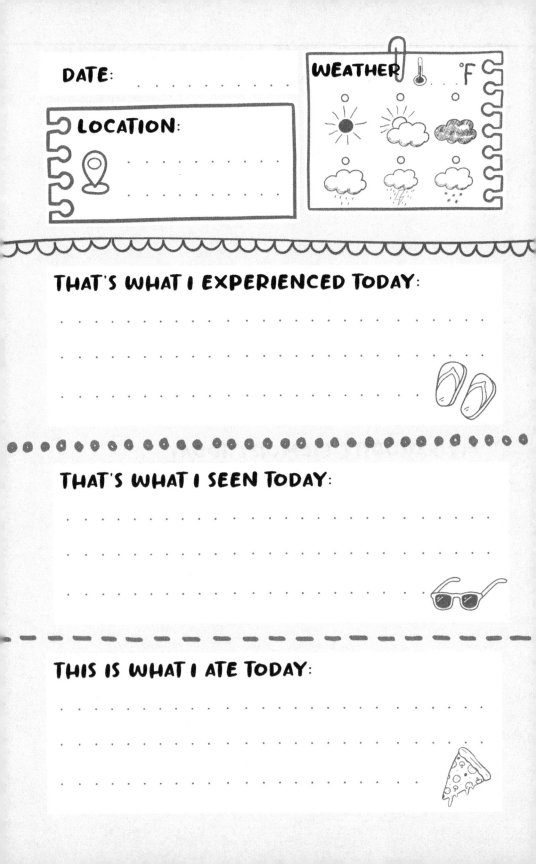

THAT'S WHAT I EXPERIENCED TODAY:

. . . .

. . . .

. . . .

THAT'S WHAT I SEEN TODAY:

. . . .

. . . .

. . . .

THIS IS WHAT I ATE TODAY:

. . . .

. . . .

. . . .

DRAW WHAT YOU HAVE EXPERIENCED TODAY:

OR INSERT PHOTOS, ENTRY CARDS OR STAMPS

MY FAVORITE MEMORY TODAY

. . . .

. . . .

I AM GRATEFUL FOR THAT TODAY

. . . .

. . . .

THIS IS HOW MY DAY WAS TODAY

DATE: . . . .

WEATHER 🌡 . . . . °F

LOCATION: . . . .
. . . .

THAT'S WHAT I EXPERIENCED TODAY:

. . . .

. . . .

. . . .

THAT'S WHAT I SEEN TODAY:

. . . .

. . . .

. . . .

THIS IS WHAT I ATE TODAY:

. . . .

. . . .

DRAW WHAT YOU HAVE EXPERIENCED TODAY:

OR INSERT PHOTOS, ENTRY CARDS OR STAMPS

MY FAVORITE MEMORY TODAY

· ·

· ·

I AM GRATEFUL FOR THAT TODAY

· ·

· ·

THIS IS HOW MY DAY WAS TODAY

DATE: . . . .

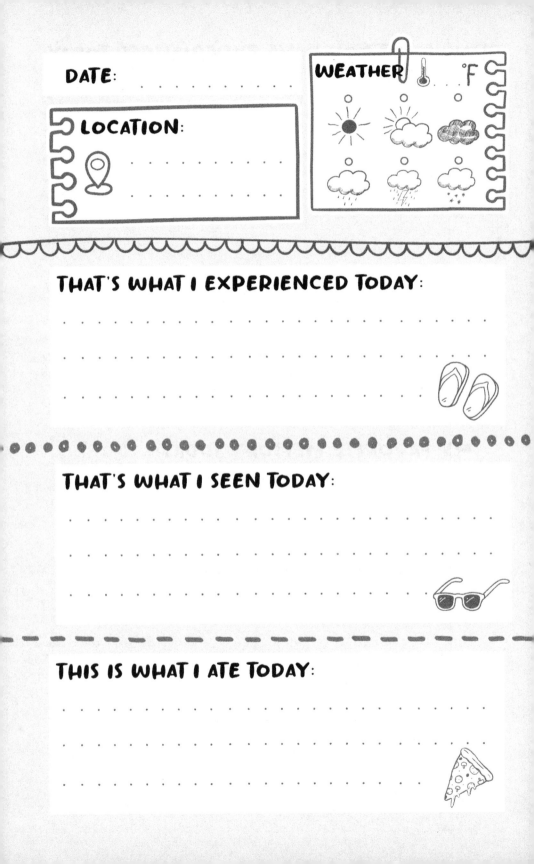

WEATHER °F

LOCATION: . . . .

THAT'S WHAT I EXPERIENCED TODAY:

. . . .

. . . .

. . . .

THAT'S WHAT I SEEN TODAY:

. . . .

. . . .

. . . .

THIS IS WHAT I ATE TODAY:

. . . .

. . . .

. . . .

DRAW WHAT YOU HAVE EXPERIENCED TODAY:

OR INSERT PHOTOS, ENTRY CARDS OR STAMPS

MY FAVORITE MEMORY TODAY

· ·

· ·

I AM GRATEFUL FOR THAT TODAY

· ·

· ·

THIS IS HOW MY DAY WAS TODAY

DATE: . . . .

WEATHER  . . . . °F

LOCATION: . . . .

. . . .

THAT'S WHAT I EXPERIENCED TODAY:

. . . .

. . . .

. . . .

THAT'S WHAT I SEEN TODAY:

. . . .

. . . .

. . . .

THIS IS WHAT I ATE TODAY:

. . . .

. . . .

. . . .

DRAW WHAT YOU HAVE EXPERIENCED TODAY:

OR INSERT PHOTOS, ENTRY CARDS OR STAMPS

MY FAVORITE MEMORY TODAY

. . . .

I AM GRATEFUL FOR THAT TODAY

. . . .

. . . .

THIS IS HOW MY DAY WAS TODAY

DATE: . . . .

WEATHER 🌡 . . . °F

LOCATION: . . . .

THAT'S WHAT I EXPERIENCED TODAY:

. . . .

. . . .

. . . .

THAT'S WHAT I SEEN TODAY:

. . . .

. . . .

. . . .

THIS IS WHAT I ATE TODAY:

. . . .

. . . .

. . . .

DRAW WHAT YOU HAVE EXPERIENCED TODAY:

OR INSERT PHOTOS, ENTRY CARDS OR STAMPS

MY FAVORITE MEMORY TODAY

I AM GRATEFUL FOR THAT TODAY

THIS IS HOW MY DAY WAS TODAY

DATE: . . . .

WEATHER 🌡 . . . °F

LOCATION: . . . .
📍 . . . .

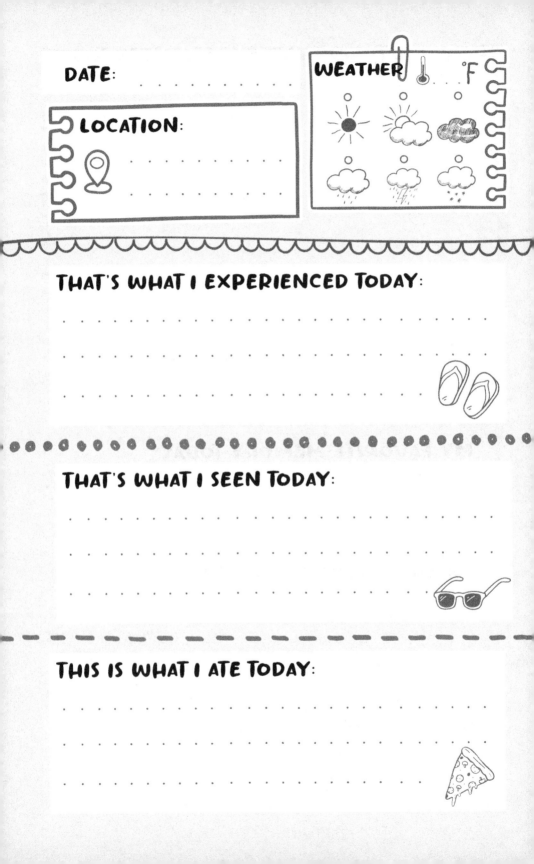

THAT'S WHAT I EXPERIENCED TODAY:

. . . .

. . . .

. . . .

THAT'S WHAT I SEEN TODAY:

. . . .

. . . .

. . . .

THIS IS WHAT I ATE TODAY:

. . . .

. . . .

. . . .

DRAW WHAT YOU HAVE EXPERIENCED TODAY:

OR INSERT PHOTOS, ENTRY CARDS OR STAMPS

MY FAVORITE MEMORY TODAY

. . . .

I AM GRATEFUL FOR THAT TODAY

. . . .

THIS IS HOW MY DAY WAS TODAY

DATE: . . . .

WEATHER  . . . . °F

LOCATION:

. . . .

. . . .

THAT'S WHAT I EXPERIENCED TODAY:

. . . .

. . . .

. . . .

THAT'S WHAT I SEEN TODAY:

. . . .

. . . .

. . . .

THIS IS WHAT I ATE TODAY:

. . . .

. . . .

. . . .

DRAW WHAT YOU HAVE EXPERIENCED TODAY:

OR INSERT PHOTOS, ENTRY CARDS OR STAMPS

MY FAVORITE MEMORY TODAY

. . . .

. . . .

I AM GRATEFUL FOR THAT TODAY

. . . .

. . . .

THIS IS HOW MY DAY WAS TODAY

DATE: . . . .

WEATHER 🌡 . . . . °F

LOCATION: . . . .
. . . .

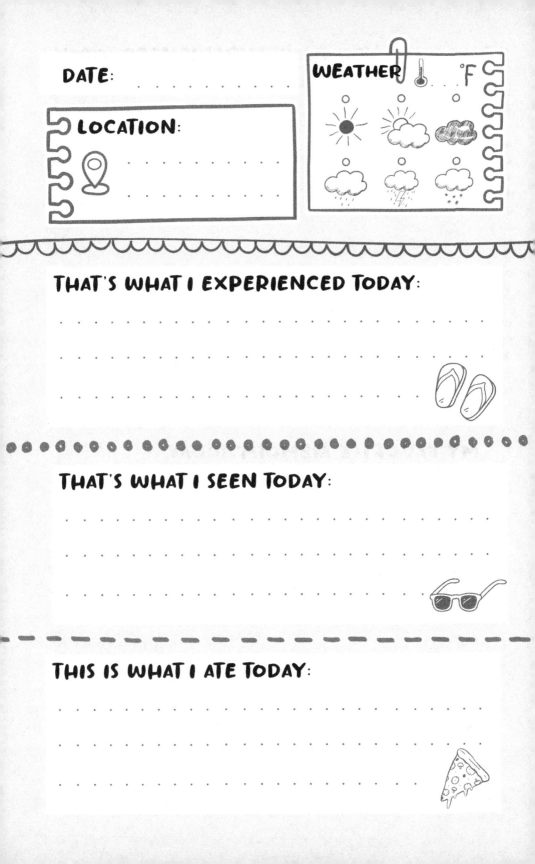

THAT'S WHAT I EXPERIENCED TODAY:

. . . .

. . . .

. . . .

THAT'S WHAT I SEEN TODAY:

. . . .

. . . .

. . . .

THIS IS WHAT I ATE TODAY:

. . . .

. . . .

. . . .

DRAW WHAT YOU HAVE EXPERIENCED TODAY:

OR INSERT PHOTOS, ENTRY CARDS OR STAMPS

MY FAVORITE MEMORY TODAY

. . . .

. . . .

I AM GRATEFUL FOR THAT TODAY

. . . .

. . . .

THIS IS HOW MY DAY WAS TODAY

DATE: . . . .

WEATHER  °F

LOCATION: . . . .

. . . .

THAT'S WHAT I EXPERIENCED TODAY:

. . . .

. . . .

. . . .

THAT'S WHAT I SEEN TODAY:

. . . .

. . . .

. . . .

THIS IS WHAT I ATE TODAY:

. . . .

. . . .

DRAW WHAT YOU HAVE EXPERIENCED TODAY:

OR INSERT PHOTOS, ENTRY CARDS OR STAMPS

MY FAVORITE MEMORY TODAY

. . . .

. . . .

I AM GRATEFUL FOR THAT TODAY

. . . .

. . . .

THIS IS HOW MY DAY WAS TODAY

DATE: . . . .

WEATHER 🌡 . . . °F

LOCATION: . . . .

THAT'S WHAT I EXPERIENCED TODAY:

. . . .

THAT'S WHAT I SEEN TODAY:

. . . .

THIS IS WHAT I ATE TODAY:

. . . .

DRAW WHAT YOU HAVE EXPERIENCED TODAY:

OR INSERT PHOTOS, ENTRY CARDS OR STAMPS

MY FAVORITE MEMORY TODAY

I AM GRATEFUL FOR THAT TODAY

THIS IS HOW MY DAY WAS TODAY

DATE: . . . .

WEATHER 🌡 . . . °F

LOCATION: . . . .
. . . .

THAT'S WHAT I EXPERIENCED TODAY:

. . . .

. . . .

. . . .

THAT'S WHAT I SEEN TODAY:

. . . .

. . . .

. . . .

THIS IS WHAT I ATE TODAY:

. . . .

. . . .

. . . .

DRAW WHAT YOU HAVE EXPERIENCED TODAY:

OR INSERT PHOTOS, ENTRY CARDS OR STAMPS

MY FAVORITE MEMORY TODAY

I AM GRATEFUL FOR THAT TODAY

THIS IS HOW MY DAY WAS TODAY

DATE: . . . .

LOCATION: . . . .

WEATHER . . . °F

THAT'S WHAT I EXPERIENCED TODAY:

. . . .

. . . .

. . . .

THAT'S WHAT I SEEN TODAY:

. . . .

. . . .

. . . .

THIS IS WHAT I ATE TODAY:

. . . .

. . . .

DRAW WHAT YOU HAVE EXPERIENCED TODAY:

OR INSERT PHOTOS, ENTRY CARDS OR STAMPS

MY FAVORITE MEMORY TODAY

. . . .

. . . .

I AM GRATEFUL FOR THAT TODAY

. . . .

. . . .

THIS IS HOW MY DAY WAS TODAY

DATE: . . . .

WEATHER . . . . °F

LOCATION: . . . .
. . . .

THAT'S WHAT I EXPERIENCED TODAY:

. . . .
. . . .
. . . .

THAT'S WHAT I SEEN TODAY:

. . . .
. . . .
. . . .

THIS IS WHAT I ATE TODAY:

. . . .
. . . .
. . . .

DRAW WHAT YOU HAVE EXPERIENCED TODAY:

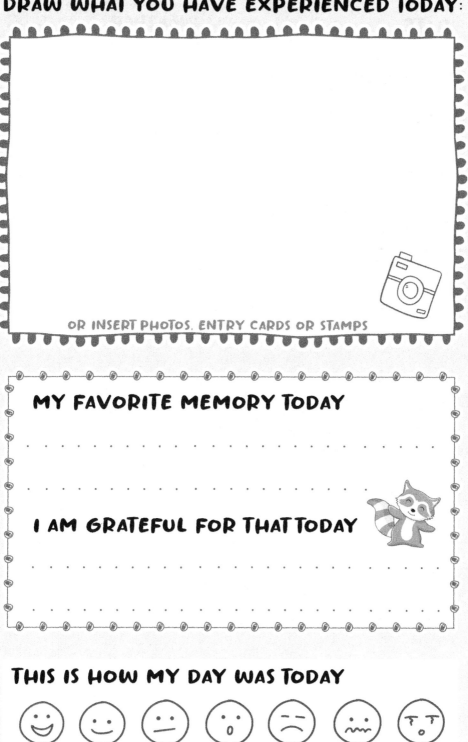

OR INSERT PHOTOS, ENTRY CARDS OR STAMPS

MY FAVORITE MEMORY TODAY

. . . .

. . . .

I AM GRATEFUL FOR THAT TODAY

. . . .

. . . .

THIS IS HOW MY DAY WAS TODAY

DATE: . . . .

WEATHER 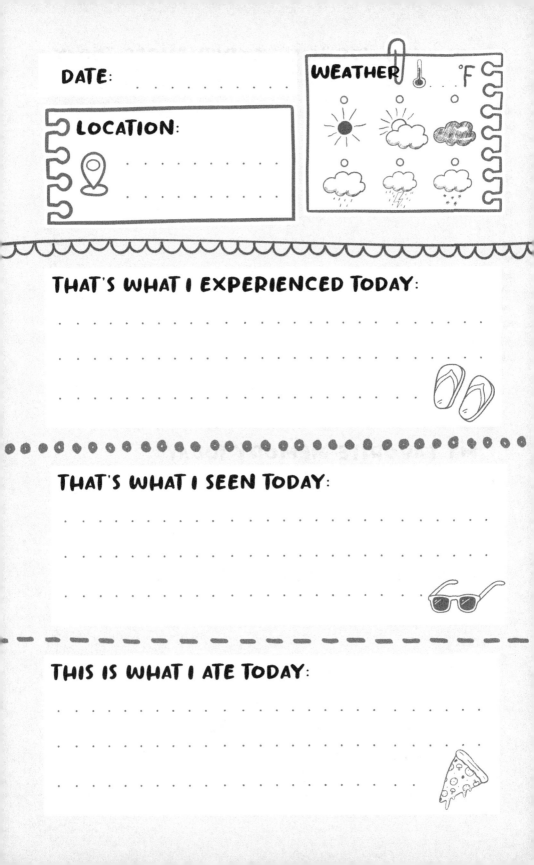 °F

LOCATION:

THAT'S WHAT I EXPERIENCED TODAY:

THAT'S WHAT I SEEN TODAY:

THIS IS WHAT I ATE TODAY:

DRAW WHAT YOU HAVE EXPERIENCED TODAY:

OR INSERT PHOTOS, ENTRY CARDS OR STAMPS

MY FAVORITE MEMORY TODAY

. . . .

. . . .

I AM GRATEFUL FOR THAT TODAY

. . . .

. . . .

THIS IS HOW MY DAY WAS TODAY

DATE: . . . .

WEATHER °F

LOCATION: . . . .

THAT'S WHAT I EXPERIENCED TODAY:

. . . .

. . . .

. . . .

THAT'S WHAT I SEEN TODAY:

. . . .

. . . .

. . . .

THIS IS WHAT I ATE TODAY:

. . . .

. . . .

. . . .

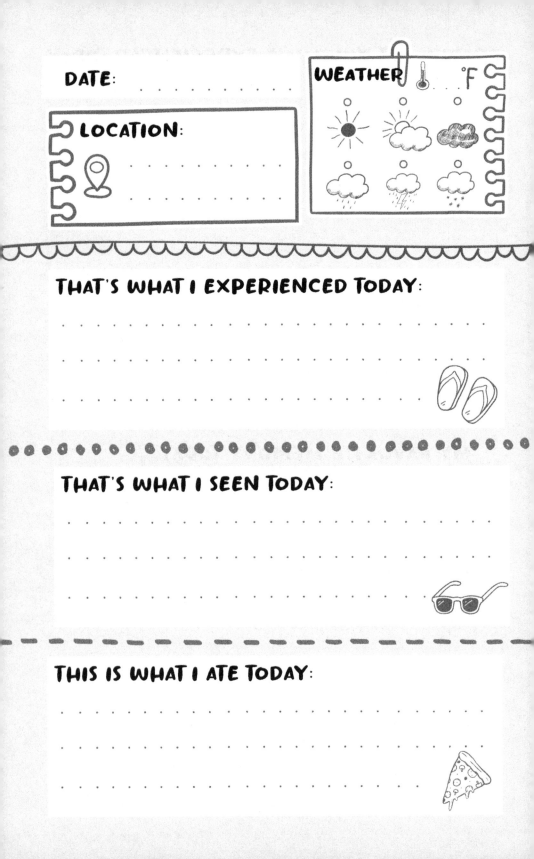

DRAW WHAT YOU HAVE EXPERIENCED TODAY:

OR INSERT PHOTOS, ENTRY CARDS OR STAMPS

MY FAVORITE MEMORY TODAY

. . . .

I AM GRATEFUL FOR THAT TODAY

. . . .

THIS IS HOW MY DAY WAS TODAY

DATE: . . . .

WEATHER 🌡 . . . °F

LOCATION:
📍 . . . .
. . . .

THAT'S WHAT I EXPERIENCED TODAY:

. . . .
. . . .
. . . .

THAT'S WHAT I SEEN TODAY:

. . . .
. . . .
. . . .

THIS IS WHAT I ATE TODAY:

. . . .
. . . .
. . . .

DRAW WHAT YOU HAVE EXPERIENCED TODAY:

OR INSERT PHOTOS, ENTRY CARDS OR STAMPS

MY FAVORITE MEMORY TODAY

· ·

· ·

I AM GRATEFUL FOR THAT TODAY

· ·

· ·

THIS IS HOW MY DAY WAS TODAY

DATE: . . . .

WEATHER 🌡️ . . . . . °F

LOCATION:

📍 . . . .

. . . .

THAT'S WHAT I EXPERIENCED TODAY:

. . . .

. . . .

. . . .

THAT'S WHAT I SEEN TODAY:

. . . .

. . . .

. . . .

THIS IS WHAT I ATE TODAY:

. . . .

. . . .

. . . .

DRAW WHAT YOU HAVE EXPERIENCED TODAY:

OR INSERT PHOTOS, ENTRY CARDS OR STAMPS

MY FAVORITE MEMORY TODAY

· ·

· ·

I AM GRATEFUL FOR THAT TODAY

· ·

· ·

THIS IS HOW MY DAY WAS TODAY

DATE: . . . .

WEATHER 🌡 . . . . . °F

LOCATION: . . . .
. . . .

THAT'S WHAT I EXPERIENCED TODAY:

. . . .

. . . .

. . . .

THAT'S WHAT I SEEN TODAY:

. . . .

. . . .

. . . .

THIS IS WHAT I ATE TODAY:

. . . .

. . . .

. . . .

DRAW WHAT YOU HAVE EXPERIENCED TODAY:

OR INSERT PHOTOS, ENTRY CARDS OR STAMPS

MY FAVORITE MEMORY TODAY

. . . .

. . . .

I AM GRATEFUL FOR THAT TODAY

. . . .

. . . .

THIS IS HOW MY DAY WAS TODAY

DATE: . . . .

LOCATION:

. . . .

. . . .

WEATHER °F

THAT'S WHAT I EXPERIENCED TODAY:

. . . .

. . . .

. . . .

THAT'S WHAT I SEEN TODAY:

. . . .

. . . .

. . . .

THIS IS WHAT I ATE TODAY:

. . . .

. . . .

. . . .

DRAW WHAT YOU HAVE EXPERIENCED TODAY:

OR INSERT PHOTOS, ENTRY CARDS OR STAMPS

MY FAVORITE MEMORY TODAY

. . . .

. . . .

I AM GRATEFUL FOR THAT TODAY

. . . .

. . . .

THIS IS HOW MY DAY WAS TODAY

DATE: . . . .

WEATHER 🌡 . . . °F

LOCATION: . . . .
. . . .

THAT'S WHAT I EXPERIENCED TODAY:

. . . .
. . . .
. . . .

THAT'S WHAT I SEEN TODAY:

. . . .
. . . .
. . . .

THIS IS WHAT I ATE TODAY:

. . . .
. . . .
. . . .

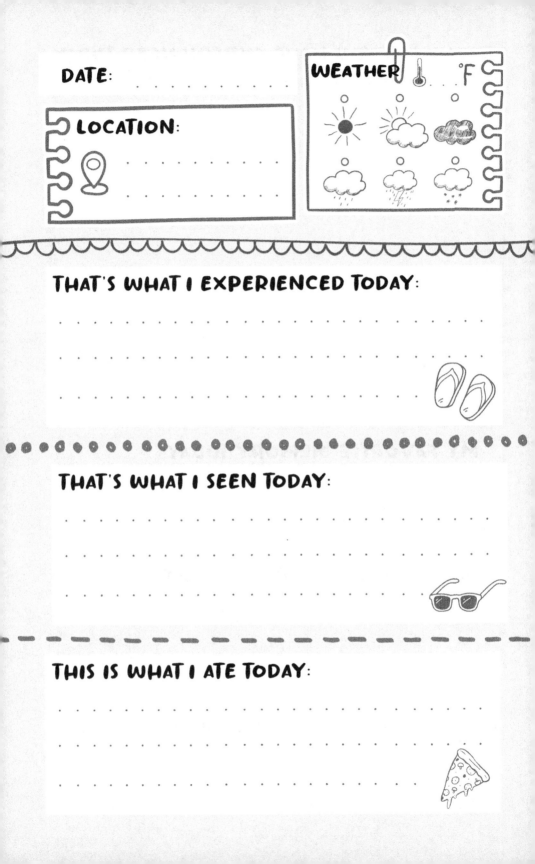

DRAW WHAT YOU HAVE EXPERIENCED TODAY:

OR INSERT PHOTOS, ENTRY CARDS OR STAMPS

MY FAVORITE MEMORY TODAY

. . . .

. . . .

I AM GRATEFUL FOR THAT TODAY

. . . .

. . . .

THIS IS HOW MY DAY WAS TODAY

DATE: . . . .

WEATHER  . . . . °F

LOCATION: . . . .

THAT'S WHAT I EXPERIENCED TODAY:

. . . .

. . . .

. . . .

THAT'S WHAT I SEEN TODAY:

. . . .

. . . .

. . . .

THIS IS WHAT I ATE TODAY:

. . . .

. . . .

. . . .

DRAW WHAT YOU HAVE EXPERIENCED TODAY:

OR INSERT PHOTOS, ENTRY CARDS OR STAMPS

MY FAVORITE MEMORY TODAY

. . . .

I AM GRATEFUL FOR THAT TODAY

. . . .

. . . .

THIS IS HOW MY DAY WAS TODAY

DATE: . . . .

WEATHER  . . . °F

LOCATION: . . . .

. . . .

THAT'S WHAT I EXPERIENCED TODAY:

. . . .

. . . .

. . . .

THAT'S WHAT I SEEN TODAY:

. . . .

. . . .

. . . .

THIS IS WHAT I ATE TODAY:

. . . .

. . . .

. . . .

DRAW WHAT YOU HAVE EXPERIENCED TODAY:

OR INSERT PHOTOS, ENTRY CARDS OR STAMPS

MY FAVORITE MEMORY TODAY

. . . .

. . . .

I AM GRATEFUL FOR THAT TODAY

. . . .

. . . .

THIS IS HOW MY DAY WAS TODAY

DATE: . . . .

WEATHER . . . °F

LOCATION: . . . .

THAT'S WHAT I EXPERIENCED TODAY:

. . . .

. . . .

. . . .

THAT'S WHAT I SEEN TODAY:

. . . .

. . . .

. . . .

THIS IS WHAT I ATE TODAY:

. . . .

. . . .

. . . .

DRAW WHAT YOU HAVE EXPERIENCED TODAY:

OR INSERT PHOTOS, ENTRY CARDS OR STAMPS

MY FAVORITE MEMORY TODAY

· · · · · · · · · · · · · · · · · ·

· · · · · · · · · · · · · · · · · ·

I AM GRATEFUL FOR THAT TODAY

· · · · · · · · · · · · · · · · · ·

· · · · · · · · · · · · · · · · · ·

THIS IS HOW MY DAY WAS TODAY

DATE: . . . .

WEATHER 🌡 . . . . °F

LOCATION: . . . .

. . . .

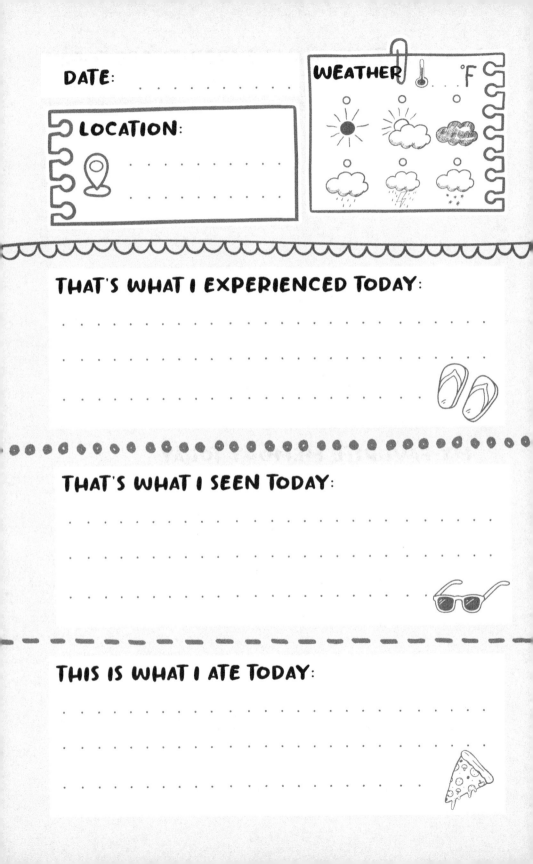

THAT'S WHAT I EXPERIENCED TODAY:

. . . .

. . . .

. . . .

THAT'S WHAT I SEEN TODAY:

. . . .

. . . .

. . . .

THIS IS WHAT I ATE TODAY:

. . . .

. . . .

DRAW WHAT YOU HAVE EXPERIENCED TODAY:

OR INSERT PHOTOS, ENTRY CARDS OR STAMPS

MY FAVORITE MEMORY TODAY

. . . .

. . . .

I AM GRATEFUL FOR THAT TODAY

. . . .

. . . .

THIS IS HOW MY DAY WAS TODAY

DATE: . . . .

WEATHER 🌡 . . . . °F

LOCATION: . . . .
. . . .

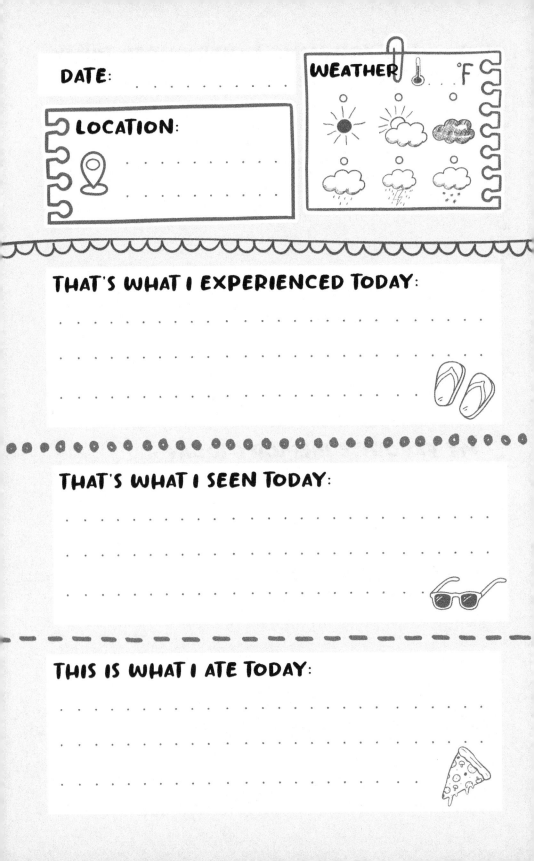

THAT'S WHAT I EXPERIENCED TODAY:

. . . .

. . . .

. . . .

THAT'S WHAT I SEEN TODAY:

. . . .

. . . .

. . . .

THIS IS WHAT I ATE TODAY:

. . . .

. . . .

. . . .

DRAW WHAT YOU HAVE EXPERIENCED TODAY:

OR INSERT PHOTOS, ENTRY CARDS OR STAMPS

MY FAVORITE MEMORY TODAY

. . . .

. . . .

I AM GRATEFUL FOR THAT TODAY

. . . .

. . . .

THIS IS HOW MY DAY WAS TODAY

DATE: . . . .

WEATHER  . . . . °F

LOCATION:

. . . .

. . . .

THAT'S WHAT I EXPERIENCED TODAY:

. . . .

. . . .

. . . .

THAT'S WHAT I SEEN TODAY:

. . . .

. . . .

. . . .

THIS IS WHAT I ATE TODAY:

. . . .

. . . .

. . . .

DRAW WHAT YOU HAVE EXPERIENCED TODAY:

OR INSERT PHOTOS, ENTRY CARDS OR STAMPS

MY FAVORITE MEMORY TODAY

. . . .

. . . .

I AM GRATEFUL FOR THAT TODAY

. . . .

. . . .

THIS IS HOW MY DAY WAS TODAY

DATE: . . . .

LOCATION: . . . .

WEATHER . . . . °F

THAT'S WHAT I EXPERIENCED TODAY:

. . . .

. . . .

. . . .

THAT'S WHAT I SEEN TODAY:

. . . .

. . . .

. . . .

THIS IS WHAT I ATE TODAY:

. . . .

. . . .

. . . .

DRAW WHAT YOU HAVE EXPERIENCED TODAY:

OR INSERT PHOTOS, ENTRY CARDS OR STAMPS

MY FAVORITE MEMORY TODAY

I AM GRATEFUL FOR THAT TODAY

THIS IS HOW MY DAY WAS TODAY

DATE: . . . .

WEATHER 🌡 . . . . °F

LOCATION: . . . .

THAT'S WHAT I EXPERIENCED TODAY:

. . . .

. . . .

. . . .

THAT'S WHAT I SEEN TODAY:

. . . .

. . . .

. . . .

THIS IS WHAT I ATE TODAY:

. . . .

. . . .

. . . .

DRAW WHAT YOU HAVE EXPERIENCED TODAY:

OR INSERT PHOTOS, ENTRY CARDS OR STAMPS

MY FAVORITE MEMORY TODAY

. . . .

I AM GRATEFUL FOR THAT TODAY

. . . .

THIS IS HOW MY DAY WAS TODAY

DATE: . . . .

LOCATION:

. . . .

. . . .

WEATHER 🌡 . . . °F

THAT'S WHAT I EXPERIENCED TODAY:

. . . .

. . . .

. . . .

THAT'S WHAT I SEEN TODAY:

. . . .

. . . .

. . . .

THIS IS WHAT I ATE TODAY:

. . . .

. . . .

. . . .

DRAW WHAT YOU HAVE EXPERIENCED TODAY:

OR INSERT PHOTOS, ENTRY CARDS OR STAMPS

MY FAVORITE MEMORY TODAY

. . . .

. . . .

I AM GRATEFUL FOR THAT TODAY

. . . .

. . . .

THIS IS HOW MY DAY WAS TODAY

DATE: . . . .

WEATHER 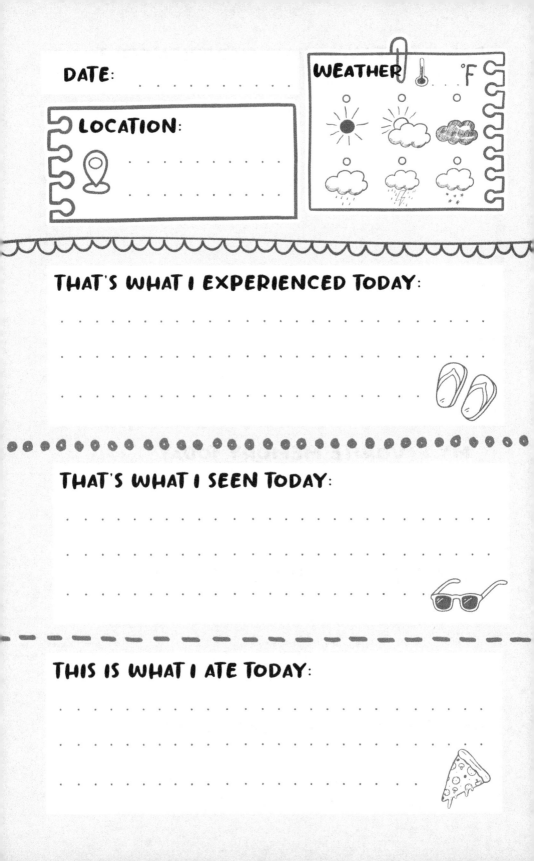 °F

LOCATION: . . . .

THAT'S WHAT I EXPERIENCED TODAY:

. . . .

. . . .

. . . .

THAT'S WHAT I SEEN TODAY:

. . . .

. . . .

. . . .

THIS IS WHAT I ATE TODAY:

. . . .

. . . .

. . . .

DRAW WHAT YOU HAVE EXPERIENCED TODAY:

OR INSERT PHOTOS, ENTRY CARDS OR STAMPS

MY FAVORITE MEMORY TODAY

. . . .

. . . .

I AM GRATEFUL FOR THAT TODAY

. . . .

. . . .

THIS IS HOW MY DAY WAS TODAY

DATE: . . . .

WEATHER 🌡 . . . °F

LOCATION: . . . .

THAT'S WHAT I EXPERIENCED TODAY:

. . . .

. . . .

. . . .

THAT'S WHAT I SEEN TODAY:

. . . .

. . . .

. . . .

THIS IS WHAT I ATE TODAY:

. . . .

. . . .

. . . .

DRAW WHAT YOU HAVE EXPERIENCED TODAY:

OR INSERT PHOTOS, ENTRY CARDS OR STAMPS

MY FAVORITE MEMORY TODAY

. . . .

. . . .

I AM GRATEFUL FOR THAT TODAY

. . . .

. . . .

THIS IS HOW MY DAY WAS TODAY

DATE: . . . .

WEATHER 🌡 . . . °F

LOCATION: . . . .
. . . .

THAT'S WHAT I EXPERIENCED TODAY:

THAT'S WHAT I SEEN TODAY:

THIS IS WHAT I ATE TODAY:

DRAW WHAT YOU HAVE EXPERIENCED TODAY:

OR INSERT PHOTOS, ENTRY CARDS OR STAMPS

MY FAVORITE MEMORY TODAY

· ·

· ·

I AM GRATEFUL FOR THAT TODAY

· ·

· ·

THIS IS HOW MY DAY WAS TODAY

DATE: . . . .

WEATHER 🌡 . . . . **°F**

LOCATION: . . . .

. . . .

THAT'S WHAT I EXPERIENCED TODAY:

. . . .

. . . .

. . . .

THAT'S WHAT I SEEN TODAY:

. . . .

. . . .

. . . .

THIS IS WHAT I ATE TODAY:

. . . .

. . . .

DRAW WHAT YOU HAVE EXPERIENCED TODAY:

OR INSERT PHOTOS, ENTRY CARDS OR STAMPS

MY FAVORITE MEMORY TODAY

. . . .

. . . .

I AM GRATEFUL FOR THAT TODAY

. . . .

. . . .

THIS IS HOW MY DAY WAS TODAY

DATE: . . . .

WEATHER °F

LOCATION: . . . .

THAT'S WHAT I EXPERIENCED TODAY:

THAT'S WHAT I SEEN TODAY:

THIS IS WHAT I ATE TODAY:

DRAW WHAT YOU HAVE EXPERIENCED TODAY:

OR INSERT PHOTOS, ENTRY CARDS OR STAMPS

MY FAVORITE MEMORY TODAY

. . . .

. . . .

I AM GRATEFUL FOR THAT TODAY

. . . .

. . . .

THIS IS HOW MY DAY WAS TODAY

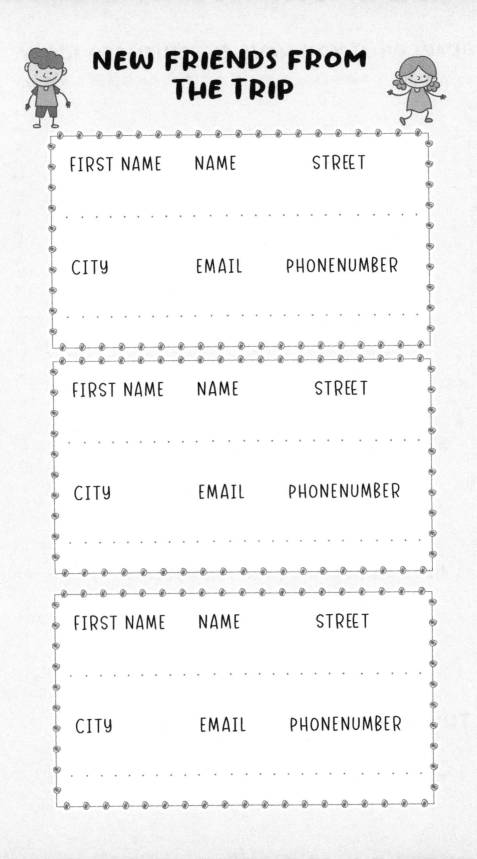

NEW FRIENDS FROM THE TRIP

FIRST NAME   NAME   STREET

· ·

CITY   EMAIL   PHONENUMBER

· ·

FIRST NAME   NAME   STREET

· ·

CITY   EMAIL   PHONENUMBER

· ·

FIRST NAME   NAME   STREET

· ·

CITY   EMAIL   PHONENUMBER

· ·

NEW FRIENDS FROM THE TRIP

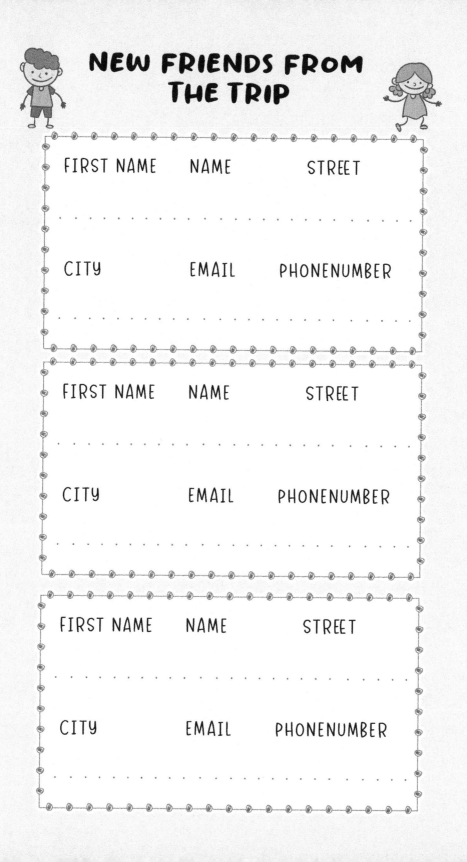

FIRST NAME   NAME   STREET

. . . .

CITY   EMAIL   PHONENUMBER

. . . .

FIRST NAME   NAME   STREET

. . . .

CITY   EMAIL   PHONENUMBER

. . . .

FIRST NAME   NAME   STREET

. . . .

CITY   EMAIL   PHONENUMBER

. . . .

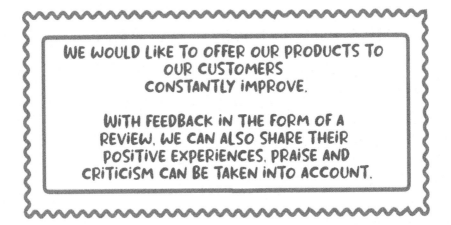

WE WOULD LiKE TO OFFER OUR PRODUCTS TO
OUR CUSTOMERS
CONSTANTLY iMPROVE.

WiTH FEEDBACK iN THE FORM OF A
REVIEW, WE CAN ALSO SHARE THEiR
POSiTiVE EXPERiENCES. PRAiSE AND
CRiTiCiSM CAN BE TAKEN iNTO ACCOUNT.

Contact
Björn Meyer
Rönnehof 5
30457 Hannover, Germany
Override2000@gmx.de
Cover design: Björn Meyer
Design elements: vecteezy.com
www.creativefabrica.com

Made in the USA
Middletown, DE
21 July 2022